SU

& ANALYSIS

OF

FACT FUL NESS

Ten Reasons We're
Wrong about the World
– and Why Things Are
Better Than You Think

A GUIDE TO THE BOOK
BY HANS ROSLING

BY *ZIP*READS

TABLE OF CONTENTS

Key Takeaway: Our negative opinions of the world are fueled by "mega misconceptions."
Key Takeaway: Instead of rich and poor, the world should be divided into four distinct income levels.
Key Takeaway: There are several different contributors to the gap instinct

Key Takeaway: No matter how you look at it, the world has objectively, dramatically improved.
Key Takeaway: The negativity instinct is driven by three forces.
Key Takeaway: Things can be both bad and better.

Key Takeaway: The world population is not just increasing and increasing.
Key Takeaway: Not all lines are straight, but some are.....

Key Takeaway: There are far fewer plane crashes than ever before; there are fewer global conflicts, far fewer deaths in those conflicts, and far fewer deaths from natural disasters.
Key Takeaway: When we're afraid, we don't see things clearly.

Key Takeaway: Frightening and dangerous are two different things.

CHAPTER 5: THE SIZE INSTINCT 25

Key Takeaway: To control the size instinct, you must compare and divide.
Key Takeaway: Use the 80/20 rule to make sense of large sets of data

CHAPTER 6: THE GENERALIZATION INSTINCT 27

Key Takeaway: Generalizations can lead to missed business opportunities.
Key Takeaway: Fight your own generalizations through travel.
Key Takeaway: Similarities in lifestyle are based far more strongly on income level than religion, culture, or nationality.

CHAPTER 7: THE DESTINY INSTINCT 30

Key Takeaway: Cultures can change over time.
Tips for Fighting the Destiny Instinct

CHAPTER 8: THE SINGLE PERSPECTIVE INSTINCT 32

Key Takeaway: Experts are only experts in their field, and sometimes they're wrong about that, too.
Key Takeaway: The Single Perspective limits possibility. ...

CHAPTER 9: THE BLAME INSTINCT 34

Key Takeaway: Pointing the finger at someone is an easy way to not solve a problem.
Key Takeaway: Institutions, regular people, and technology are responsible for most of the positive change in the world.

SYNOPSIS

In *Factfulness: Ten Reasons We're Wrong about the World — and Why Things Are Better Than You Think,* medical doctor, educator, and statistician Hans Rosling teams up with his son and daughter-in-law to challenge commonly-held notions that the world is worse off than it was in the past. His mission is for everyone to embrace a "fact-based" existence, using "factfulness" to guide every action—from watching the nightly news to solving world hunger.

Rosling presents the reader with a simple, fact-based quiz to help determine how skewed your world view may be. The responses to this quiz, he soon reveals, show that the majority of people in wealthy countries all over the world believe the rest of the world is worse off than they actually are. This "overdramatic worldview" is what he so vehemently argues against. He shows that extreme poverty has been slashed, access to healthcare and education is widely increasing, and that mortality rates have fallen precipitously.

Rosling provides endless troves of data (more than 20 percent of the original text consists of notes and references) along with personal anecdotes to make his case. The book is well-organized into ten simple "mega misconceptions" that inform our drastically misinformed beliefs. With each of these misconceptions, he clearly lays out how it affects our perceptions of reality and how we can counter it in our daily lives. The ten misconceptions are: gap, negativity, straight line, fear, size, generalization, destiny, single, blame, and urgency.

Rosling begs the reader to fight these instincts and use the power of data to inform decisions, to look beyond the doom and gloom of the news, and to see the world for what it is: an objectively better place than it has ever been before.

INTRODUCTION

In order to frame the book, Rosling presents the reader with a 13-question quiz. This quiz he has given to students, to professors, to ambassadors, to humanitarians and Nobel Laureates. You can find the official 2018 quiz at this link: http://forms.gapminder.org/s3/test-2018.

1. In all low-income countries across the world today, how many girls finish primary school?

☐ A: 20 percent ☐   B: 40 percent ☐   C: 60 percent

2. Where does the majority of the world population live?

☐ A: Low-income   countries ☐ B: Middle-income countries ☐   C: High-income countries

3. In the last 20 years, the proportion of the world population living in extreme poverty has …

☐ A: almost doubled ☐   B: remained more or less the same ☐ C: almost halved

4. What is the life expectancy of the world today?

☐ A: 50 years ☐   B: 60 years ☐   C: 70 years

5. There are 2 billion children in the world today, aged 0 to 15 years old. How many children will there be in the year 2100, according to the United Nations?

☐ A: 4 billion ☐ B: 3 billion ☐ C: 2 billion

6. The UN predicts that by 2100 the world population will have increased by another 4 billion people. What is the main reason?

☐ A: There will be more children (age below 15)
☐ B: There will be more adults (age 15 to 74)
☐ C: There will be more very old people (age 75 and older)

7. How did the number of deaths per year from natural disasters change over the last hundred years?

☐ A: More than doubled ☐ B: Remained about the same
☐ C: Decreased to less than half

8. There are roughly 7 billion people in the world today. Which map shows best where they live? (Each figure represents 1 billion people.) 9. How many of the world's 1-year-old children today have been vaccinated against some disease?

☐ A: 20 percent ☐ B: 50 percent ☐ C: 80 percent

10. Worldwide, 30-year-old men have spent 10 years in school, on average. How many years have women of the same age spent in school?

☐ A: 9 years ☐ B: 6 years ☐ C: 3 years

11. In 1996, tigers, giant pandas, and black rhinos were all listed as endangered. How many of these three species are more critically endangered today?

☐ A: Two of them ☐ B: One of them ☐ C: None of them

12. How many people in the world have some access to electricity?

☐ A: 20 percent ☐ B: 50 percent ☐ C: 80 percent

13. Global climate experts believe that, over the next 100 years, the average temperature will …

☐ A: get warmer ☐ B: remain the same ☐ C: get colder

Here are the correct answers: 1: C, 2: B, 3: C, 4: C, 5: C, 6: B, 7: C, 8: A, 9: C, 10: A, 11: C, 12: C, 13: A

(Rosling, pp. 3-5, Flatiron Books).

Well, how did you do? Chances are, you didn't do very well. In fact, the average human scores just 2 out of 13 on this test. In theory, the average chimpanzee would get 4 out of 13 just by guessing. And the tendency is for people to assume the world is much worse off than it is. Why is that? Why do some of the smartest people in the world working in fields relevant to these questions still not get the answers right? Rosling spends the rest of the book explaining the 10 reasons why a chimpanzee will likely outscore you on this test, and what you can do to fight it.

CHAPTER 1: THE GAP INSTINCT

Rosling opens the book by challenging your misconceptions about the state of the world. He argues that most people believe the world can be split simply into two sides: the rich and the poor, us and them, developed and under-developed countries, Western and non-Western nations, etc. But these delineations are not only misleading, they're patently false. This penchant to divide things into two distinct groups is what he refers to as "The Gap Instinct."

Key Takeaway: Our negative opinions of the world are fueled by "mega misconceptions."

These mega misconceptions apply to everything from child mortality rates (which are significantly lower in every single country in the world since the 1960s) to population growth. During the middle of the 20th century, the world and the data could be neatly divided into developed and developing countries, but in the past 20 years, things have changed. Poverty worldwide has more than halved and 75 percent of people today live in middle-income countries. The way we believe the world to be is an outdated concept of reality. This "gap instinct"—the concept that the world can be divided into two distinct groups—is the first of the mega misconceptions Rosling tackles.

Rosling utilizes the quiz to continuously illustrate just how widespread these incorrect beliefs are. Most people believe that people in less developed countries are illiterate, starving, uneducated, and have limited access to water and healthcare.

The reality is exactly the opposite. Only in the world's poorest countries (think less than 2 percent of the population) are things still this bad; only 9 percent of the entire world lives in low-income countries to begin with.

Key Takeaway: Instead of rich and poor, the world should be divided into four distinct income levels.

Rosling created his own scale based on dollars of income earned per day and provides illustrative examples of what each of these levels looks like in daily life. How do they get their water? What does their bedroom look like? What is their mode of transportation? Through the data you can see the large majority of the planet lives in the two middle income brackets, a billion more (roughly) live in the highest bracket, and another billion in the lowest bracket.

LEVEL 1: EXTREME POVERTY ($1 PER DAY)

· You walk miles to fetch water with a bucket every day

· You eat the same porridge for dinner every night

· You have no access to healthcare, electricity, or toilets

· Roughly 1 billion people live at this level

LEVEL 2: LOWER MIDDLE INCOME ($2 – $8 PER DAY)

- You can afford more buckets to fetch water, the water source is closer, perhaps you own a bicycle

- You can afford to cook meat, eggs, and food you didn't grow yourself

- You have intermittent access to electricity

- You have limited access to medicine and healthcare

- You may have a mattress instead of sleeping on the floor

- Roughly 3 billion people live like this today

LEVEL 3: UPPER MIDDLE INCOME ($8 – $32 PER DAY)

- You have access to tap water

- You have stable electricity

- You may have a motorbike

- You may have some savings, and could afford medicine if someone in your family got sick

- Roughly 2 billion people live like this today

LEVEL 4: WEALTHY ($32+ DOLLARS PER DAY)

- If you're reading this book, you're most likely Level 4

- You have a car, hot and cold tap water, a fridge full of food, probably a Wi-Fi connection, and you have been on an airplane on vacation

- Roughly 1 billion people live like this today

Key Takeaway: There are several different contributors to the gap instinct

Averages can be misleading—make sure to look at the more granular data.

Comparing extremes can be tempting, but most of the reality happens in the middle.

Relative poverty in your wealthy country is not the same thing as extreme poverty in other countries. Some Level 4s may be "poor" to you because they drive a beat-up car or live in a bad part of town. This is a misleading concept of poverty. Most the people in the United States living "below the poverty line" are still Level 4s on a worldwide basis.

"Factfulness is … recognizing when a story talks about a gap, and remembering that this paints a picture of two separate groups, with a gap in between. The reality is often not polarized at all" (Rosling, p. 46).

CHAPTER 2: THE NEGATIVITY INSTINCT

The second mega misconception is the negativity instinct, also known as negativity bias. This is our tendency to remember bad things more strongly than good things and thus be forever inclined to believe things are getting worse. The vast majority of respondents choose answers indicating that the world is getting worse. But the data don't support that.

- In the year 1800, 85 percent of the world lived on Level 1, in extreme poverty

- In the year 1800, life expectancy was around 30 years old, it's now over 70 years worldwide

- Until 1966, extreme poverty was the rule, not the exception

Key Takeaway: No matter how you look at it, the world has objectively, dramatically improved.

Rosling presents 32 different charts to make his case for the objective improvement of the world as a whole.

Legal slavery, oil spills, cost of solar panels, HIV infections, children dying, deaths in battle, countries with the death penalty, leaded gasoline, plane crash deaths, child labor, deaths from disaster, nuclear arms, smallpox, smoke emissions, ozone depletion, and hunger—all of these things have decreased dramatically in almost every country.

And here are 16 good things that are on the rise: new movies, protected nature reserves, women's suffrage, new music, science publications, harvest yields, literacy, democracy, child cancer survival, girls in school, monitored species, electricity coverage, mobile phones, water, internet, and immunization.

Key Takeaway: The negativity instinct is driven by three forces.

Misremembering of the past: Humans have a tendency to believe that the past was better than it was, which in turn makes the present seem worse than it is.

Selective reporting: The old news adage, "if it bleeds it leads" is true for a reason. No one is interested in news about how well things are going. One of the clearest examples of this is violent crime in America. Despite violent crime rates being on the decline for decades, most Americans believe crime is at an all-time high.

Feeling, not thinking: People don't want to admit the world is getting better because it feels like ignoring all the problems that still exist and pretending everything is OK. You can recognize that things have improved while still acknowledging there is more work to be done.

Key Takeaway: Things can be both bad and better.

In order to fight your negativity bias, you must realize that things can be both bad in some ways and still better than they used to be. You must look at the past with objectivity and fight the natural tendency to only remember the good. You must expect the negativity that comes through the media as a tool of their reporting, not an indicator of the health of society. You must remember that good news is often not reported on at all.

CHAPTER 3: THE STRAIGHT LINE INSTINCT

Rosling describes the straight line instinct as the tendency to believe that trends will increase in a straight line, just as they have in the past. Of course, this is erroneous. Many trends can be exponential, others can taper off for various reasons. Not all graphs and charts can be extended in a straight line from where the data stops. We may grow three feet in our first three years of life, but we aren't forty feet tall in our forties! Our instinct is to assume that straight lines will continue, which can lead us to a variety of incorrect conclusions.

Key Takeaway: The world population is not _just_ increasing and increasing.

Yes, the world population is currently increasing. However, it is not _just_ increasing. UN experts predict that in 2100, there will be 2 billion children on the planet: the same number that there are today. This is possible because of the precipitous drop in children born per woman around the world: from 5 children in 1965 to just 2.5 today.

As more people escape extreme poverty and gain access to education and contraception that number will continue to decline. Though it seems counterintuitive, reducing child mortality effectively _lowers_ the population growth rate. Women in countries with lower child mortality have fewer babies, because fewer of them will die. The countries with the highest number of births per woman are the countries with the highest levels of child mortality.

Key Takeaway: Not all lines are straight, but some are.

Rosling uses several examples to help remind the reader that charts come in all different shapes and sizes. While some lines are pretty straight—the relationship between income and life expectancy is basically linear, as is education and income—other trends take other shapes.

The relationship between income and literacy, for example, is an S shape. Literacy is very low in extreme poverty, shoots up as populations move into Level 2 and Level 3, and then flattens out as they enter Level 4. That is to say, by the time you reach Level 3, basically everyone is literate, and there aren't significant gains left to be made. This goes for vaccinations and owning a refrigerator as well. Yet another curve Rosling describes as a "hump"—traffic deaths increase as countries enter Level 2 or 3 and more people start to travel by motorbike, and then decrease again as countries enter Level 4 where they experience significant increases in safety regulation and education.

Lastly, is the exponential curve or "doubling line." This shape is applicable to the spread of *E. coli* bacteria (they can double every day) as well as to income spent on transportation, and miles travelled annually. As income increases, these figures will continue to double, and double again.

The doubling of income is also an important concept to understand: doubling your income from $1 a day to $2 a day drastically changes your life. Adding that extra dollar of income to a Level 4 household (going from $64 to $65 a day) makes no difference at all. Each level of income of the four levels as described by Rosling is double the previous one. And any time your income doubles (if you go from $32 to $64 per day) your standard of living will significantly increase. As he states, "This is how money works."

CHAPTER 4: THE FEAR INSTINCT

"Our natural fears of violence, captivity, and contamination make us systematically overestimate these risks" (Rosling, p. 123).

Of all the filters our brain uses to process things, things that invoke fear have the power to pass through those filters. Being afraid is a survival instinct, and our bodies needed to listen to fear in order to stay alive when we were hunting and gathering. This explains why news networks love fear mongering so much, and why it works so well for their ratings. We are programmed to pay attention to fear, even if that fear is no longer as necessary for survival as it was in humanity's past.

Key Takeaway: There are far fewer plane crashes than ever before; there are fewer global conflicts, far fewer deaths in those conflicts, and far fewer deaths from natural disasters.

Unsurprisingly, the data disagree with our common perception of how dangerous the world is. Fewer people are dying in earthquakes and tsunamis because wealthier countries have better infrastructure and stronger building codes. With more money comes better preparedness on a household level as well. Fewer people die in plane crashes because we collectively began studying and regulating aviation to avoid accidents. The world has never seen peace like that which has existed since the end of World War II. In the conflicts that do exist, fewer people are dying than in previous conflicts in the last century. But watching the news might have you believe otherwise.

Key Takeaway: When we're afraid, we don't see things clearly.

Irrational fear has led to the anti-vaccination movement, to a fear of any and all chemicals (even ones that may be good for food production and human health) and a fear of nuclear contamination—all things which have no basis in fact. Rosling describes this baseless fear of all chemicals as "chemophobia."

When we are afraid, we overlook facts. We exchange evidence-based rationality for fear-driven, knee-jerk reactions. The best way to decide if something is harmful or not is to look at the data. Nuclear power plants, even when they melt down, don't kill people. The WHO has reviewed the insecticide DDT and found it has more benefits than drawbacks. Vaccines do not cause autism, and genetically modified crops are not harmful to humans. Before you react, ask yourself if you're afraid of something and then look for the data to confirm or deny its potential harm.

Key Takeaway: Frightening and dangerous are two different things.

When something is frightening, it is a perceived danger. Terrorism, plane crashes, nuclear fallout, and murder are all frightening, but they are all *very* unlikely to happen to you.

When something is dangerous, it is a legitimate threat to your well-being. We need to consciously shift our focus from the frightening to the dangerous. Diarrhea causes far more deaths worldwide than war and the destruction of the ocean floors is a much larger threat than all the plane crashes combined. These are real, fact-based dangers we should be focusing our attention on instead of scary, but statistically unlikely, scenarios.

CHAPTER 5: THE SIZE INSTINCT

"In the deepest poverty, you should never do anything perfectly. If you do you are stealing resources from where they can be better used"
- Ingegerd Rooth

Rosling shares a story from his time working as a doctor in Mozambique. If he were to have treated every patient with the standard of care in Western countries, even more children would have died. Spending that much time on each patient was unethical; it was better for him to quickly treat as many patients as possible. But as humans, our instinct is to see the individual over the larger, often invisible, data.

Key Takeaway: To control the size instinct, you must compare and divide.

When faced with any number—it doesn't matter what it is—it is meaningless unless it is compared to another number. Big numbers will always look big, until you compare them to an even larger big number, which can give you perspective on how small that first big number really is.

4.2 million dead babies in 2016 sounds like a startlingly high number. But when you compare it to 2015 at 4.4 million, we see it's decreasing. When you compare it to the 14.4 million dead babies of 1950, it starts to seem impressive.

Raw numbers, even when compared, don't always show the whole picture. Dividing can get us a *rate* of child mortality that helps to compare apples to apples. In 1950, 97 million children were born, and 14.4 million died. This tells us the mortality rate was 15 percent. In 2016, the total number of children born was 141 million. Dividing 4.2 million by 141 million gives us a mortality rate of only 3 percent! From that perspective, the decrease is even more significant.

Key Takeaway: Use the 80/20 rule to make sense of large sets of data

The 80/20 rule states that for most things, 80 percent of the output or meaning will come from 20 percent of the input. Rosling uses the example of the world's energy sources. The world generates energy from biofuels, coal, gas, geothermal, hydro, nuclear, oil, solar and wind. Sounds like a lot. But 87 percent of the energy comes from just 3 sources: oil, coal, and gas. Whenever you have a big list of numbers, find the ones that are the most significant in order to understand which changes would have the most impact.

CHAPTER 6: THE GENERALIZATION INSTINCT

Generalization is necessary for humans to function. Generalizations give structure to the way we see the world and make it easier to make decisions. Unfortunately, generalizations can also distort our world view when we incorrectly assume two countries' cultures are the same when they are very different. Or when we assume they are very different when they are more alike than we know.

When you hear words like gang banger, soccer mom, inner city, or middle class, a wealth of preconceived notions come to mind. Try to recognize when you're generalizing in order to analyze if your often-helpful generalizations have become harmful stereotypes.

Key Takeaway: Generalizations can lead to missed business opportunities.

Rosling uses the question about vaccination—one he says is the lowest-scoring question of them all—to make a point about investment in developing nations. 88 percent of all the world's children have at least one vaccination, though most people guess 20 percent or 50 percent. In order to deliver vaccines, they must be kept cool through a complicated distribution network. The exact same distribution networks required for vaccines are used to build a factory. So, this widely believed generalization that most people don't have vaccines means that businesses are overlooking investment opportunities in countries they believe are poorer and less developed than they actually are.

"The number of people living on Level 3 will increase from 2 billion to 4 billion between now and 2040" (Rosling, p. 149).

Those living on Level 1 cannot afford a toothbrush. Many living on Level 2 share one toothbrush with the whole family. On Level 3, everyone owns their own toothbrush. Women on Level 2 can begin to afford feminine hygiene products.

The populations still living in extreme poverty are rising out of it, and the opportunities to market products to those increasing their income from $8 a day to $16 a day are being vastly underestimated. Fully developed countries are practically saturated with consumer products, and the successful corporations of the next two decades will be the ones who shift their focus to Africa and Asia.

Key Takeaway: Fight your own generalizations through travel.

The more you experience the world first-hand, the more you can break existing stereotypes. You may think of Uganda as a country where everyone is living in squalor and there is no infrastructure, but of course, that is only one part of the picture.

If you cannot afford to travel, Rosling's daughter-in-law, Anna Rosling Rönnlund, created Dollar Street (http://https://www.gapminder.org/dollar-street/): a project to help people understand what life on Levels 1, 2, and 3, and 4 looks like. The website is full of comparative photos of everything from toothbrushes to cooking utensils to show you how different income levels around the world live.

Key Takeaway: Similarities in lifestyle are based far more strongly on income level than religion, culture, or nationality.

If you are currently living on Level 2, no matter where in the world you live, it is likely that your house has a patchwork roof, that you share a toothbrush among multiple family members, that your toilet has walls, (though it is still a pit latrine), and you heat water in an iron pot on a tripod over a fire.

Understanding these similarities is key to fighting your generalization instinct. People who live in huts don't do so because it's their culture, they do so because of their income level. People with half-built brick homes in poorer countries don't do so because they are lazy; they buy bricks as a way of investing their money since cash can be stolen and they don't have access to bank accounts.

Before you assume an aspect of someone's life is a "cultural thing," and therefore a divisive thing, dig a little deeper to understand the *why* behind it.

CHAPTER 7: THE DESTINY INSTINCT

"[The destiny instinct] makes us believe that our false generalizations from chapter 6, or the tempting gaps from chapter 1, are not only true, but fated: unchanging and unchangeable." (Rosling, p. 167).

The destiny instinct leads people to believe that Africa will never develop (Africa is a vastly diverse continent of 54 countries and a billion people!) or that Islamic countries are fundamentally different than Christian countries, that they will always be "backwards." These ideas are of course, not true. Africa is developing at an incredible pace, and many parts of Africa live on Levels 3 and 4. The Islamic world is developing as well. Iran has an even lower birth rate than the United States—an indicator that is strongly tied to income and education—and saw the fastest decrease in birth rate in the entire world in the 1980s.

Key Takeaway: Cultures can change over time.

The destiny instinct has us thinking that cultures will always hold the same ideals. Religious people will have more babies (false), a country that doesn't support abortion legalization now never will (also false). One of the drivers of these changes can be an increase in income. As we know, increased income leads to increased education, which can lead to increased women's rights and a decrease in patriarchal social structures. These patriarchic views aren't culturally based—they're antiquated and income-based.

Tips for Fighting the Destiny Instinct

· Recognize that slow change is still change

· Remember that just because something was true five years ago, doesn't mean it is still true

· Talk to older generations to get a sense of how far cultural values have changed

CHAPTER 8: THE SINGLE PERSPECTIVE INSTINCT

The single perspective instinct is the desire to find simple solutions to problems. We want there to be a single cause of a problem because then the solution is quite simple: be against the cause. Simple problems are easy to explain, to fix, and to understand. The single perspective instinct makes us dig our heels into our political leanings because we don't want to acknowledge that a situation is more complicated, more nuanced, or more bi-partisan.

Key Takeaway: Experts are only experts in their field, and sometimes they're wrong about that, too.

Be sure to take the wisdom of experts with a grain of salt: some experts and Nobel laureates scored worse on the quiz than the average citizen. Experts also can exaggerate the direness of causes to which they have devoted themselves. For example, a scientist who works for the conservation of endangered species is likely to overestimate the decline of certain animal populations. This very negativity is a rallying cry for their cause, but it overlooks all the progress that has been made.

Key Takeaway: The Single Perspective limits possibility.

Approaching issues with a single perspective (equality is better than inequality, free markets are better than communism) runs the risk of blocking out potential benefits from the other side. Most solutions are complicated and complex, and you can't say definitively one system is always better than the other. Generally speaking, equality is better than inequality, but not all things that cause inequality are bad. Just like not all communist countries are worse in every way than capitalist ones.

Rosling uses Cuba and the United States as a pointed example. Though Cuba is a communist country, they actually have better healthcare and a healthier population than the United States. They are "the poorest of the healthy countries." The United States is very rich, but also has objectively worse health care than most other wealthy nations—they spend twice as much money per capita to have a shorter lifespan. The U.S. is the "sickest of the rich."

A central government can't solve all of its people's problems any more than a free market can solve all of *its* people's problems. The best solutions lie in opening your mind to the possibility that a seemingly opposing ideology may have something valuable to add.

CHAPTER 9: THE BLAME INSTINCT

"To understand most of the world's significant problems we have to look beyond a guilty individual and to the system" (Rosling, p. 207).

Key Takeaway: Pointing the finger at someone is an easy way to not solve a problem.

There are groups that we are used to blaming for problems in the world: evil corporations, journalists, the media, or foreigners. We are seldom capable of pointing that finger at ourselves. The reality is that most of the negative things in the world are more complicated than a single villain: most are caused by complicated systems and interactions. When we assign blame to a single actor, we stop looking for a cause to the problem; we think we've found it.

We tend to blame the media for making the world seem so terrible. They are presenting a skewed world view, true, but only because they are subject to the same mega misconceptions we all are. It's easy to blame India and China with their 2 billion people for driving up CO_2 emissions, but in reality, the richest billion people in the world are responsible for more than half of the world's CO_2 emissions. And most of those people don't live in India or China. We can't expect poorer countries not to develop just because we got to develop first.

Key Takeaway: Institutions, regular people, and technology are responsible for most of the positive change in the world.

Institutions and people don't get as much praise as they deserve. Most big things aren't put into action by a single person just as most negative changes aren't fueled by a single, evil dictator (with some notable exceptions). Whether placing blame or assigning credit ("blame or claim"), look for a system; try to understand the complicated reasons behind how you got to where you are. More often than not, there won't be a simple answer or a single finger to point. And getting to the bottom of those convoluted explanations is the only way to really solve a problem.

CHAPTER 10: THE URGENCY INSTINCT

"When we are afraid and under time pressure and thinking of worst-case scenarios, we tend to make really stupid decisions" (Rosling, p. 226).

Rosling shares one of his more personally traumatic stories to illustrate how dangerous the urgency instinct can be. While working as a doctor in Mozambique, the district was overcome with a deadly paralytic disease. Not knowing whether or not it was contagious, he made a rash decision to throw up a road block, stopping anyone else from entering the area.

This road block, however, meant that the women and children taking the bus into town were unable to sell their goods. So instead of taking the bus, they found a boat to take them. The boat was unsafe, capsized, and all the mothers, children, and fishermen drowned. The moral of the story is had he thought through the potential consequences of closing the road, he could have easily realized that locals would still find a way to get into town. Instead, the *urgency* of the situation made him feel that he had to make a decision, any decision, and fast.

Key Takeaway: The urgency instinct is frequently abused by sales people and activists, and it's almost never true.

Buy now! Act Fast! This deal won't last!

Any time you hear phrasing like that, it is playing to your urgency instinct. It makes us want to do something, to take action. We feel the same way when there is a disaster or immediate danger. But acting quickly in these situations is almost always a bad idea. Our urgency instinct is best used to jump out of the way of moving traffic or run from a lion, not to solve climate change.

Distorting data to make a problem seem direr ultimately hurts the cause. Environmentalism is a noble and necessary cause, but scaring people into believing things are worse than they are doesn't help the planet or the movement. Use the data, rather than your emotions, to make calculated decisions.

Key Takeaway: There are five potential mega killers threatening the globe today.

Rosling lists these threats as global pandemic, financial collapse, world war, climate change, and extreme poverty. We must do everything in our power to fight against these evils. While global pandemic, financial collapse, and world war are difficult to predict because they are so complex, climate change and extreme poverty are two things we have already seen, and we already know how to fix. The key to solving these problems going forward is international cooperation.

CHAPTER 11: FACTFULNESS IN PRACTICE

Rosling closes the book by reviewing his suggestions for factfulness and telling us how we can move forward to become more factful. Not only must we pay attention in our lives, be diligent in recognizing our mega misconceptions and in adjusting them, but we must do the same for our children.

We need to teach our children the truth of the world today along with an accurate vision of the past. We need to provide them context for the progress the world has made while still being clear about the current threats. We should be teaching our children both humility and curiosity, so they always want to learn more and never let their own presumed knowledge get in the way. Teach them to be open-minded and willing to change their opinion when presented with new information. Being able to admit you don't know something is one of the wisest things you can do.

The reasons the humans scored worse than theoretical chimpanzees on Rosling's quiz is because the information we think we know is working against us. All of our mega misconceptions are getting in the way of the truth, and we don't know how to see through them.

Rosling implores you to apply these techniques to everything—not just your world view, but to your job, your community, to local politics. We are swimming in misconceptions and acting on instincts because no one ever stops to ask, "What do the data say about that?"

EDITORIAL REVIEW

In *Factfulness*, Rosling makes a strong case that things are better off than they used to be. After all, it's hard to disagree with all that data and those pretty charts. But more so than making the argument that the world is better, he attempts to help us understand *why* we think it's worse, and how we can change that. Humans are innately prone to bias, but that doesn't mean we can't fight it. Rosling avoids calling himself an optimist (and has been criticized by some as a "Pollyannist") but is rather a self-described "possibilist"— he neither hopes without reason nor fears without reason.

The ten misconceptions that lead to misinformed conclusions are clearly laid out, easy to follow, and conveniently distilled into useful tips at the end of each chapter. He uses the power of data in concert with the power of personal stories to illustrate each misconception in action.

As a personal testament, Rosling is no more immune to these misconceptions than anyone else. Most of these are tales of errors he committed himself, some of which caused the deaths of dozens of people, or potentially the deaths of thousands. These do not weigh on him lightly, and they provide meaningful context for the arguments he's making. Each time this happened, he was forced to evaluate why he made the mistake that he did and how he could avoid it in the future.

Whether or not your day job may impact the lives of thousands of people, the advice is still worth taking. We are inundated with negative stories in the news, from activists, and politicians. We are led to believe things are worse than they are because it's better for ratings, better for the cause, or better for a person's political career.

Rosling stays carefully away from any political leanings, insisting that bias is a bipartisan issue and that progress will only be made by lessening political divides, not widening them. And the best way to bridge that gap is for everyone to take his advice, fight their own biases, and use the data to make correct, informed, rational, reasonable decisions.

BACKGROUND ON AUTHOR

Hans Rosling was a Swedish physician and statistician who used computer software and props, as well as his own showmanship, to illuminate facts and trends revealed by data that people were often unwilling to see. These lectures made him a YouTube star, and you can watch his most popular lecture, titled "The Best Stats You've Ever Seen" here: https://www.ted.com/talks/hans_rosling_shows_the_best_stats_you_ve_ever_seen.

Rosling studied statistics and medicine at Uppsala University in Sweden and public health at St. John's Medical College in Bangalore, India. One of his greatest achievements was the discovery of a previously unidentifiable paralytic disease in rural Africa caused by the consumption of under-processed cassava roots. In *Factfulness*, he states that discovery transformed him from being a district doctor to a researcher, and he spent the next 10 years of his life studying the interplay between economies, societies, toxins, and food.

In 2005, Rosling founded the Gapminder foundation with his son, Ola Rosling, and his daughter-in-law, Anna Rosling Rönnlund. Both Ola and Anna made significant contributions to this book and to the life's work of Hans, often crunching the numbers and developing the materials for Hans' TED Talks.

Hans received numerous awards throughout his life including being named one of *Time* Magazine's Most

Influential People of 2012 and receiving the Harvard Humanitarian Award that same year.

Hans Rosling passed away from pancreatic cancer in February 2017, just before the release of *Factfulness*. It is his first full-length book and the culmination of his life's work.

END OF BOOK SUMMARY

*If you enjoyed this **ZIP Reads** publication, we encourage you to purchase a copy of the original book from.*

We'd also love an honest review on Amazon.com!

Made in the USA
Lexington, KY
29 August 2018